MW00892982

Color Your Mind: A Psychedelic Coloring Book for Grown-Ups

A Mindful Coloring Adventure for Serenity, Calmness and Relaxation

Dear Colorist,

Welcome to *Color Your Mind: A Psychedelic Coloring Book for Grown-Ups*! This coloring book is designed to take you on a trippy journey through a whimsical world of vibrant colors and surrealistic designs.

Inspired by the psychedelic art movement of the 1960s, this coloring book features a range of intricate and mind-bending patterns, kaleidoscopic designs, and fantastical scenes that are sure to inspire your creativity and take you on a groovy trip down memory lane.

Whether you're looking to relax and unwind after a long day, or just want to let your imagination run wild, this coloring book is the perfect way to tap into your inner artist and let your mind expand beyond the boundaries of reality.

So grab your colored pencils or crayons, and get ready for a groovy adventure transporting you to a world of color and creativity. We can't wait to see what colorful masterpieces you'll create!
Happy coloring!

To achieve optimal results, we recommend placing a sheet of paper or thin cardboard behind the page you're coloring. This will prevent bleed-through onto the pages behind it.

50 Shades of Emotions: A Coloring Book for the Soul © Technicoloring, 2023
Art by: Matt Hoffman

First Edition 2023

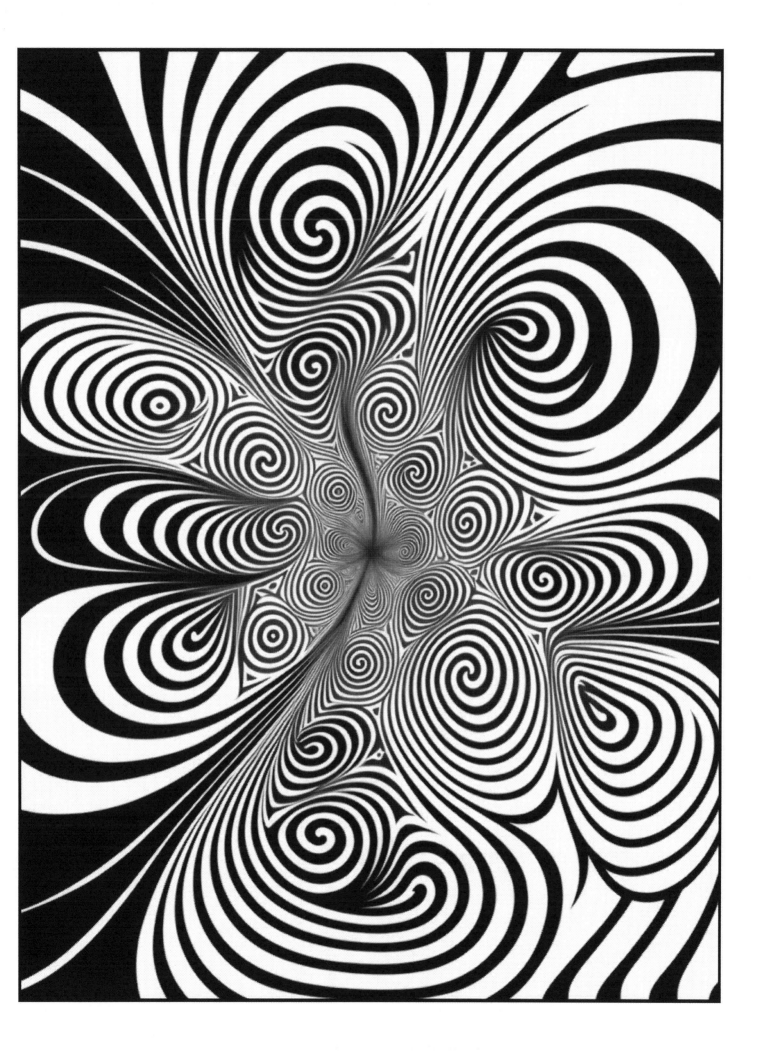

Made in the USA
Columbia, SC
16 December 2024